Top left: Stephenson 2-2-2 Patentee of 1834. This was a direct descendant of the 0-2-2 Rocket of 1829 and 2-2-0 Planet of 1830. Two cylinders were mounted beneath the smokebox, the whole enclosed by outside sandwich frames. Such frames were popular throughout the Victorian era as axle failures would not then necessarily result in derailment. Valves were of simple sliding bridge form, operated by Stephenson's patent cam motion.

1. regulator handle
2. firebox water space
3. firebox
4. ashpan
5. safety valve positions
6. eccentric cams
7. eccentric rods
8. connecting rod
9. boiler tubes
10. boiler
11. piston rod
12. steam heading dome
13. valve push rods
14. piston
15. main steam pipe
16. valve bridge
17. blast pipe
18. cylinder
19. steam chest
20. smoke box
21. chimney

Lower left: Churchward 4-6-0 Star class locomotive of the GWR, introduced 1907. Most of the essential features of the modern simple acting loco were present. Frames were built up from plate members through which the axles passed. Although a four cylinder type, the outside cylinder has been omitted for clarity. Piston valves operated by inside Walschaert gear.

1. fire door
2. firebox
3. clearance for axle
4. ashpan
5. firebox water space
6. brick arch
7. coupling rod
8. safety valves
9. feedwater inlet
   (clack valves)
10. boiler tubes
11. superheating tubes
12. boiler
13. eccentric cams
14. reversing coupling
15. connecting rod
16. superheating header
17. regulator (throttle)
18. main steam pipe
19. exhaust blast pipe
20. chimney (smoke stack)
21. piston rod
22. valve push rod
23. piston valves
24. smokebox
25. steam chest
26. piston
27. cylinder

(N.B. These drawings are not to scale.)

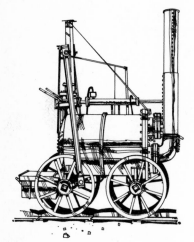

Above: Trevithick's last locomotive, 'Catch-me-who-can', that ran on a circular demonstration track in Euston for several weeks in the summer of 1808.

Opposite: Phineas Davies was noted in America for his vertically boilered anthracite burning locomotives from the 1830's. Shown is a 'Grasshopper' of the 1870's. The similar 'Crabs' and 'Muddiggers' has horizontal cylinders.

WORLD STEAM
LOCOMOTIVES

Described and illustrated by

JAMES G. ROBINS

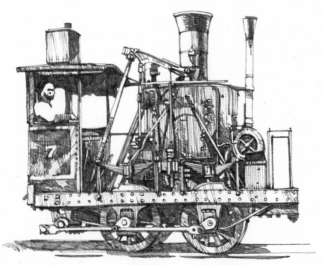

ARCO PUBLISHING COMPANY, INC.
New York

© 1973 by James G. Robins

Published 1974 by Arco Publishing Company, Inc.
219 Park Avenue South, New York, N.Y. 10003

Library of Congress Catalog Card
Number 73–80142

ISBN 0-668-03325

Printed in Great Britain

Opposite: One of a series of curious 6-2-0 Cramptons
built by Baldwins for the Camden & Amboy railway
in 1849.

CONTENTS

GREAT BRITAIN

Introduction

As might be said of the internal combustion engine, it is curious that a machine as wasteful and inefficient as the steam engine should have had such a long innings as prime mover of man and his belongings. Also that a machine with such potential for technological development should remain cast in virtually the same mould for all of its 150 years of service. The answer to both points can essentially be summed up in economics. As long as the revenue returns exceeded the cost of construction, fuel and maintenance then the machine was 'efficient'. Its basic simplicity in construction and operation only emphasising this situation. Furthermore, only those technical improvements that advanced or maintained that economic status quo were accepted as the norm.

Not that the last steam locos were primitive anachronisms, they did a job, and did it well—so long as the figures in the ledgers balanced, and so long as one considers their 'efficiency' in that light. Some locomotives were unfortunate, especially in Britain, in that they served for as little as ten years, alongside others whose service extended to thirty and forty years duration—a term which would have been well within their own capability.

However such anomalies were not the concern of the early railway companies. Fuel was cheap, as was labour. Locomotives were small, as were loads and distances, but at least business was regular and profitable. Only later would the disadvantages of this policy manifest themselves. But, just as Watt's delaying tactics might have prevented the earlier appearance of effective locomotives, it is sobering to realise that but for the Napoleonic wars forcing up the cost of horse fodder, it might have been another thirty years before the loco became an established fact.

Below: Richard Trevithick 1771-1833. As well as high pressure pump engines and locomotives, Trevithick pioneered the mechanisation of agriculture. A brilliant engineer, he was unfortunately a poor businessman, and eventually died in penury.

Left: The Coalbrookedale engine. Little is known of the machine or its operation, but being entirely unsprung it probably took a heavy toll of the brittle iron plateway on which it ran.

Above: The Newcastle engine of 1805. Apart from a revised layout, the most obvious advance was in the flanged wheels for wooden edge rail, but again without springs track damage was probably heavy.

Right: Blenkinsop's 1812 loco, showing the single cogged wheel and rack track. Although two cylinders were employed, removing the need for a cumbersome flywheel, the machine had an inefficient straight flue, and no steam blast.

Below: Hedley re-introduced the return flue and steam blast, maintaining the two cylinder format. Variously modified, his machines survived in service until 1860, and two, 'Puffing Billy' and 'Wylam Dilly', remain as museum pieces to this day.

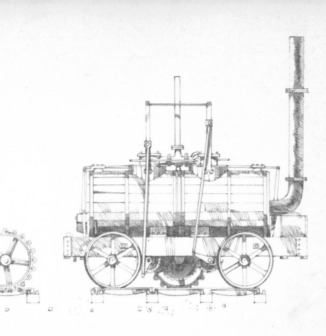

The first self-propelled steam engine, or artillery tractor built by Cugnot in Paris in 1769. Undoubtedly a step in the right direction, but entirely unsuccessful—the machines continued existence giving it a disproportionate call to fame.

In Britain, James Watt's assistant, William Murdoch, built some steam carriage models in the 1780's, only to be prevented from further experiment by Watt's erection of a barricade of patents, thereby preserving a monopoly of steam engines.

Thus it was under these circumstances Richard Trevithick developed his high pressure steam engines for tin mines. From table-top models of the 1790's he built his first full size locomotive in 1803 for the Coalbrookedale Iron works. The fire tube was U-shaped, firebox and chimney being at the same end of the boiler. Steam from a single horizontal cylinder was exhausted into the chimney, creating a forced firebox draught. Similar locos ran at Penydarren in 1804 and Newcastle in 1805, finally in London in 1808, after which Trevithick gave up through lack of support.

Under his patent in 1812 Murray and Blenkinsop built a number of locomotives for the Middleton colliery, Leeds, running on cast iron edge rail, using their own patent rack and pinion system. Two years later William Hedley built some two cylinder locos more in keeping with Trevithick's designs for the Wylam colliery. Two of them survive as museum pieces. In the same year George Stephenson built his first locomotive, 'Blucher' at Killingworth.

The importance of George and Robert Stephenson in the evolution of the worlds' railways should not be underestimated. Before them the railway was, to say the least, primitive—through their technical skill, and above all, business acumen, it was moulded into the institution we know today.

George Stephenson was born in Wylam, Newcastle in 1781. At seventeen he became enginewright to the local colliery, before moving on to Killingworth, where his first locomotive was built in 1814. In 1821 he was appointed engineer to the Stockton & Darlington Railway. From the outset he specified wrought iron edge rail to a gauge of 4 ft. 8½ in., and locomotive hauling power. At the opening in September 1825, 'Locomotion' was the only loco available, and hauled the inaugural train, although parts of the line were still horse operated. Later he engineered the Liverpool & Manchester Railway, his company's locomotives also supplying most of the motive power. Subsequently he became engineering consultant to a number of pioneer railway companies, both in England and abroad.

His son Robert joined him in 1821 at the age of eighteen. He lacked none of his father's inventive or business genius, becoming responsible for much of the design work within the Stephenson company. He was largely responsible for designing the Rocket,

Top centre: George (left) and Robert Stephenson.

Top left: Locomotion, original loco of the S & D. Although retaining an inefficient straight single flue, coupled drivers and improved valve operation gave significant advance. The distinctive wheels were fitted in 1828 by Timothy Hackworth after a boiler explosion.

Lower left: Hackworth succeeded G. Stephenson as engineer on the S & D. For freight work he introduced six-coupled locos with return flue boilers. The first was 'Royal George' in 1827.

4

Far right: The Rocket, 1829. To decide what locos to adopt the L & M railway held trials at Rainhill. Rocket was overall winner, subsequently hauling the inaugural train in 1830. Its worn out shell now rests in the Science Museum, London.

Centre: The Patentee, built in considerable numbers by Stephensons from 1834, and copied throughout the world. It created an outside frame, inside cylinder, single driver theme that lasted the rest of the century.

which, with its multi-tubular boiler—increasing the rate of evaporation and allowing automatic regulation of steam production—was a major milestone in locomotive development. It became the prototype for a long line of rapidly developing locomotives and created a precedent for the products of virtually every other locomotive company for several decades.

George Stephenson retired in 1844, and died four years later. Robert, in addition to locomotives, became recognised as a bridge engineer. He entered parliament as member for Whitby in 1847, and died in London in 1859.

Most of Britain's present railway mileage was laid during the 'Boom' between 1840 and 1870. Small companies sprang up in virtually every county, jealously guarding their sole right to haulage on their own tracks, making long journeys tedious affairs. Many were built on scandalously weak financial bases, so that eventually government control was introduced, especially over the levying of land for railways, and over the public use of them.

A factor in the land situation was the penalising of railway companies by private landowners to minimal land usage, limiting loading gauges. The Stephensons' 4 ft. 8½ in. rail gauge was adopted as standard in most of the land, the principle exception being Brunel's 7 ft. gauge in the west, although this was brought into line in 1892.

For passenger traffic single-drivers remained the norm for rather too long, until heavier trains required more tractive effort. Another curious persistence was the absence of brakes on freight locos, which lasted until the end of steam traction.

Top left: Indicating the divergence between passenger and freight locos, Stephenson's 1846 'Long boiler' express (top) with large single drivers, and Kitson's 'Hector' long boilered goods of 1845, with six coupled wheels.

Lower left: Last of the 'single-driver' era, Stirling's elegant 4-2-2 singles for the Great Northern from 1870. Fast, but forced to double-heading on heavier trains.

Top right: Adams 4-4-0 for the London & South Western Railway from 1887. The external appearance of this type of small-boilered, un-superheated, big-wheeled loco, might be taken as typical of the era.

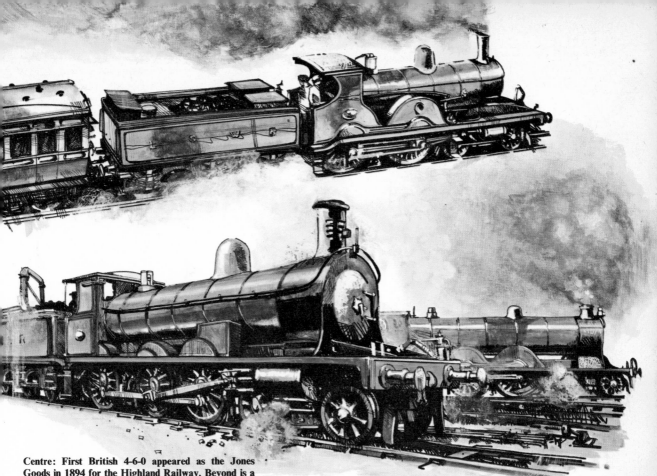

Centre: First British 4-6-0 appeared as the Jones Goods in 1894 for the Highland Railway. Beyond is a large-boilered Caledonian 4-6-0 passenger loco of 1906.

Below: H. A. Ivatt introduced the Atlantic (4-4-2) format on the Great Northern in 1898. Shown is his big-boilered Atlantic of 1904, incorporating for the first time a wide firebox and, retrospectively, super-heating.

Left: A broad gauge Pearson 4-4-0ST (Saddle Tank) on the Bristol & Exeter Line circa 1860. The huge size of broad gauge machines can be gauged from the surrounding figures. The B & E also operated some 4-2-4T express tanks, with 9 ft. driving wheels.

Right: Most famous of the Victorian tank locos, Stroudley's 0-6-0T Brighton 'Terriers' for the LBSCR from 1872. Fifty were built for S. London suburban services, so were fitted with vacuum brakes. The straw yellow colour scheme was described by Stroudley as 'improved engine green'.

Below: First articulated types to attain series production were those under the patent of Robert Fairlie. Effectively they were two locomotives with powered bogies married to a common firebox. Shown is an 1879 Fairlie 0-4-4-0T still working on the revived Ffestiniog Railway in N. Wales.

Above: Typical of many hundreds of 60 cm. gauge locos for service on the Western Front 1914-18, a Hudson 0-6-0WT (Well Tank).

From the earliest times it was British practice to use tank engines in preference to tender types for most short-line, commuter and shunting work. The need for boiler-side water tanks generally limited the size of tank types, although some, notably the Baltics (4-6-4) of the London, Brighton & South Coast railway weighed over a hundred tons and were used for express traffic. Generally mineral and industrial lines used tank types, exclusively so on narrow gauge track. It was from sources such as these that the move toward articulation began.

Left: Underground railways commenced under London in 1863. Shown is an ex-District line Beyer-Peacock 4-4-0T of 1870 in London Transport service, having been reprieved after electrification of the line in 1905. To reduce tunnel congestion exhaust steam was condensed back into the side tanks.

Above: Several railway companies introduced steam railmotors on unprofitable branchlines. These were the equivalent of an omnibus, a small steam engine being totally enclosed within the carriage body. Illustrated is a London North Western specimen circa 1905.

**Above: Gresley A.1/3 three-cylinder Pacific 'Sir Visto'
of the LNER.** All cylinders were of the simple-
expansion type, giving high power, good riding characteristics and economy. Piston valves were operated by
Walschaert rotary motion, the inner valves by Gresley's
patent link gear.

**Below: Churchward's four-cylinder simple 'Star' class,
introduced in 1907.** The later 'Castles' (1923) and
'Kings' (1927) were essentially enlarged Stars, the last
Castles being built in 1951 for British Railways. The
two-cylinder 'Halls', 'Granges' and 'Counties' also
embodied the same styling, which latterly became
distinctly dated, especially from the maintenance point
of view, but none-the-less, all were excellent machines.

**Centre: Based on the 'Lord Nelson' of the S.R., the
LMS 'Royal Scot' class was introduced in 1927** after
protracted controversy over the relative merits of
compound and simple propulsion. Designed by Sir
Henry Fowler, the 'Scot' was a 4-6-0 three-cylinder
simple design; such was the need—and confidence in
the design—that fifty were ordered off the drawing-
board, and it proved to be a most successful locomotive
type.

10

Below right: Modern motive power was initiated on the Southern by R. W. Urie from 1912, with a general superheated, two cylinder policy. The culmination of this policy was the 'King Arthur' 4-6-0 of 1925, and extended by R. E. L. Maunsell's four-cylinder 'Lord Nelson', illustrated here, of the same year. Beyond is a 'Schools' class three-cylinder 4-4-0, the last, most powerful and most celebrated 4-4-0 in Britain, derived from the 'Nelson' for the arduous Hastings line.

In 1923 the previously extant twenty-five railway companies were rationalised by act of Parliament into four major groups— Southern (SR), Great Western (GWR), London Midland & Scottish (LMSR), and London North-Eastern (LNER). The date is also indicative of the general trend towards big-power locomotives, and towards general standardisation of locomotives, systems and parts within each group, although each had initially to contend with its inherited pot pourri.

Leader in this field was the GWR which under Chief Mechanical Engineer J. G. Churchward had from 1907 maintained a standardised system that was to last to the end of steam traction. Eventually Churchward's principles were to influence the other groups, but not until the late twenties did they achieve universal application.

There was still a general preference for narrow firebox 4-6-0 types for express passenger work on all systems. N. H. Gresley introduced the first production Pacific (4-6-2) into the Great Northern in 1922, becoming series A.1 and A.3 in LNER service. Pacifics became pre-eminent on the LMS and SR in 1933 and 1941 respectively, but never succeeded the ten-wheelers on the GWR.

At this stage top quality coal was still reasonably cheap, the value of wide fireboxes with lower grade fuels as yet to be appreciated.

Right: O. V. S. Bullied was potentially Britain's most inventive C.M.E., but was restricted first by World War II, and later by nationalisation. He planned to cover all the Southern's mainline requirements with three Pacific classes, 'Merchant Navy', seen here as the prototype 'Channel Packet', built in 1941; 'West Country' and 'Battle of Britain', built to lighter axle loadings. To facilitate maintenance the chain driven valve gear was enclosed in an oil bath and the boiler encased. Once teething troubles were overcome they became singularly excellent locomotives. From 1956 all Merchant Navy and most of the other classes were rebuilt to more conventional lines, with Walschaert valve gear, but retaining the distinctive Box-pok wheels.

Right: W. A. Stanier, a former pupil of Churchward, succeeded Fowler on the LMS in 1931. His first Pacifics, the 'Princess' class appeared in 1933, and an improved class—the 'Coronation' in streamlined form in 1937, following the success of Gresley's A.4's on the LNER. A record of 114 m.p.h. was held by the class for a while in 1937. Initially they were painted royal blue, then as shown from 1939, but due to rising maintenance costs few survived the war in streamlined form.

It is generally recognised that the principle countries of the world achieved a peak of steam development between the two world wars. Britain was no exception. Already by the 1930's electric and diesel traction were making major inroads into steam's traditional domain, and all railway systems—no matter what form of motive power used—were suffering from advances in road and air transport. However there were areas where steam held advantages. No other system could (at that time) haul such heavy freight tonnage over long distances at such economic rates, few other

Two of the earliest applications of streamlining were on machines of unique mechanical significance, products of Gresley's fertile mind. Above top is the first of five class P.2 2-8-2's, Britain's only passenger traffic Mikadoes. 'Cock O' the North' alone had Lentz poppet valves, the rest piston valves, but proved unpopular on the Scottish routes for which they were built. After a brief period with A.4 styling all were eventually rebuilt as Pacifics. Above lower: LNER no. 10000, the only Baltic (4-6-4) tender engine in Britain, built 1929 with the Yarrow water-tube boiler, rating 450 lb. pressure, and compound cylinders. Its potential seemed high, but continued operating troubles caused it to be scrapped in 1938.

modes of transport could go so long without major overhaul, or have such potential service longevity. Early passenger diesel units were like aeroplanes in their limited seating capacity, and electric traction required such extensive trackside engineering before it became really effective.

Therefore the constantly sought after qualities of greater economy, power and speed were more necessary than ever before —plus a newer quality, prestige, to win back the wayward passenger.

And so it was that the railway companies were virtually panicked into steam's most glamorous era.

13

Top left: There were three basic austerity designs for the war department, two 2-8-0's and a 2-10-0. Several hundred of each were built under the direction of R. A. Riddles, based largely on experience of Stanier's designs. Illustrated is a 2-8-0 for home use, its weathered exterior emphasising the reduction of maintenance.

Lower left: An ex-GWR pannier tank on a branchline Auto-train in early British railways days. The carriages were of the early BR stock in red and cream livery. Auto-trains replaced Railmotors for short-line operation, with driving controls in the last carriage for push-pull work.

Centre: Most unorthodox of the austerity types were the Q1 0-6-0's designed by Bullied for the Southern. The uncompromising exterior disguised a machine of exceptional power for its size.

The advent of the Second World War had a number of significant immediate and long term effects on Britain's railways. The railway companies were brought under more direct central control, although preserving their individual identity; many formerly widespread essential materials, and available labour, became scarce; locomotives were made to haul formerly inconceivably heavy loads in both freight and passenger traffic; large numbers of American locomotives were imported, their efficiency and ruggedness having considerable influence on future constructional practise.

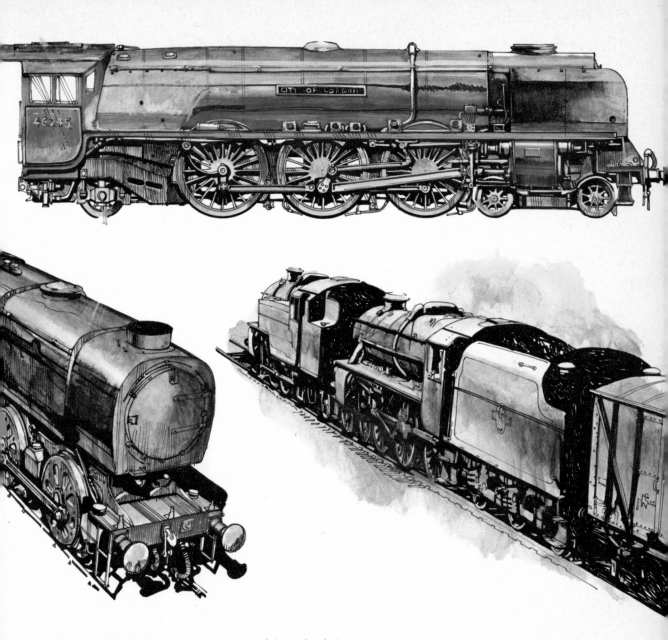

The shortage of materials led to a number of Austerity designs for use at home and abroad, using non-strategic materials, basic parts and minimal embellishments for adequate and inexpensive performance. This simplification had the added benefit of minimising maintenance requirements.

Of the existing pre-war designs, many suffered badly from reduced maintenance and lower grade fuels. Streamliners either had their cowlings removed or cut back, and many had their exquisite paintwork covered with sombre black. But all of this was not without its beneficial effects. The future efficiency of Britain's railways owed a great deal to the economies of these years.

Top right: Stanier's Duchess class Pacifics appeared in streamlined form in 1938. They survived the war in the form shown, the last two being built in modified form in 1947 by Stanier's successor, H. G. Ivatt. They remained Britain's most powerful passenger locos.

Lower right: Yet another Stanier design, the Black Five 4-6-0, seen here headed by class 4 tank on heavy freight. Although a good design the Black Five perpetuated the LMS 'small engine' policy, and had to be double-headed on even moderately heavy trains.

Top left: Typical of the types taken over from the railway companies, an ex-LNER class A3 Gresley Pacific, fitted with German style deflectors and Kylchap double exhaust in the late 1950's.

Centre: A class 4 Mogul (2-6-0) for light mixed traffic operations. Of the same basic design was a 2-6-4T, which was incorporated in the same classification.

Top right: Class 7 Britannia Pacific 'Iron Duke', decorated for the Southern Region Golden Arrow Pullman service. The similar but lighter Class 6 'Clan' Pacifics were less successful in operation, and were used exclusively on Scottish services.

Britain's railway companies were nationalised as one system in January 1948. Plans were put in hand, under the auspices of Mr. R. A. Riddles, to build a fleet of locomotives incorporating all of the best features of former company policies plus some from overseas. Additionally, the locomotives of the former companies were incorporated, still essentially in their original areas—and indeed new batches of some were built to British Railways requirements.

Sadly the scheme was first compromised, and eventually doomed by a general policy of dieselisation and electrification. The last steam loco, a class 9F 2-10-0 'Evening Star', was built at Swindon in 1960, and steam had dissappeared from revenue service by the end of the decade, some of the last built having been in service for less than five years.

There were to have been eleven classes to cover all British Railways requirements. All were designed for efficient and economic

running; to standardise the variety of types in service; and to simplify maintenance. The lower numbered classes covered both tank and tender types of 2-6-0, 2-6-4T, 2-6-2T, and 4-6-0 arrangements. These compounded Britain's unwritten 'small-loco' policy, and it might be said that there were far too many of them. Classes 6 (Clans) and 7 (Britannias) were two-cylinder passenger Pacifics. Class 8 materialised as a single three-cylinder Pacific; and class 9, a two-cylinder 2-10-0 essentially for freight duties.

All were good, but not exceptional locomotives. However, I do venture to suggest that the 251 locos built of class 9 will be seen in retrospect as Britain's finest all-round steam locomotives, powerful (by British standards, almost 40,000 lbs. tractive effort) as a freight hauler, and surprisingly fast (up to 90 m.p.h.) as a passenger type.

It's ironic that they should arrive almost too late.

EUROPE

Introduction

Below left: The Lyons-St. Etiennes Railway opened in 1827 for passenger and freight traffic, hauled by horses. Stephenson's 0-4-0 was introduced on the Givors-Rive-de-Gier section in 1828. Its probable configuration is illustrated here. It had the straight single flue of Locomotion, but the inclined cylinders of Rocket. Beyond is Seguin's first locomotive hauling coal cauldrons. Note the return flue boiler and fans on the tender with their leather connections to the firebox. The position of the cylinders between the driving wheels allowed their use as springs. Later Seguin locos were of simpler design, with steam blast and straight multi-tubular boilers.

As was the case with the former mechanisation of the textile industry, British engineers introduced the steam railway into Europe. But it is well to reflect that the first permanent ways, in the form of ruts cut in paved roads, were to be found in pre-Christian Greece and Roman Italy. Furthermore, flanged wheels and wooden rails were used in German mines early in the sixteenth century. Add to this Cugnot's steam tractor of 1769 and one can see that Britain's 'invention' of the steam locomotive was merely a technical advancement of a mode of transport long established on the Continent.

The first locomotive to run in Europe was built under Blenkinsop's patent in 1816 by the Royal Iron Foundry, Berlin. Twelve years later the Stephenson company introduced the second, an 0-4-0 for the French Lyons-St. Etienne Railway. Stephenson's Patentee type 2-2-2 was adopted by many of the earliest European railways. It was pioneer motive power in Austria, Belgium, Germany, and Russia. Modified forms by Sharps Bros., Longridge and others pioneered Danish, Italian, Dutch and Spanish railways. This monopoly led to general (but not universal) adoption of the 4 ft. 8½ in. standard rail gauge, Spain and Portugal being notable exceptions at 5 ft. 6 in.

Marc Seguin's locomotive of 1829 was the first indigenous design. It had a return flue multi-tubular boiler, but no steam blast, the firebox being inadequately draughted by two belt driven fans on the tender. Another design of note for its eccentricity was that of the Swede Munktells in 1847. Its four coupled wheels were driven from both ends of two pistons. It was a failure.

A prominent import of the 1830's was the American Norris type 4–2–0. The famous German firms of Borsig and Henschel based their first creations on this type in 1841 and 1848 respectively. The majority of early home-built locomotives were amalgamations of overseas ideas. Some of the more important engineers were also expatriates, notably Haswell, Crampton and de Glehn.

However, the most important single feature of early European railways was the amount of State control, preventing the chaos of small private companies typical of Britain and the USA, and allowing some standardisation of loading gauges etc., that was to be of considerable importance in later years.

Below right: Borsig's first design of 1841. Its kinship to the Norris type is obvious. The extra trailing axle was intended to support the weight of the firebox, spreading the total weight over a broader area of track, but it only succeeded in depriving the driving wheels of much of their tractive effort. Henschel's first design, the Drache of 1848, was similarly based on the Norris, but had a Stephenson long boiler and an extra pair of driving wheels behind the firebox, creating a much more effective 4-4-0.

Top left: Spanish 0-6-0 of the RENFE operating from Valencia in the 1960's. Many similar and 0-8-0 loco-motives were built for the NORTE from 1855 and, apart from the broad gauge, were generally similar to several hundreds built throughout western Europe. A comment on their excellence is their continued existence in revenue service, in some cases after eighty or ninety years.

Lower left: A Crampton of the Paris, Lyons and Mediterranean Railway (PLM) circa 1860. It was essentially a Stephenson longboiler made more stable by removing the driving wheels to a position behind the firebox.

Top right: A type 29 0-6-0 built for the Austrian Süd-bahn under the direction of John Haswell in 1860, seen here in service with the Graz Koflacher Eisenbahn in the 1960's. Haswell was an Englishman who arrived with the first Austrian locomotive in 1837. The cowled smokestack was a prominent feature of most early Austrian locos.

The second half of the nineteenth century was witness to greater individuality of design in the European nations, and to the birth of new principles of major importance in later years. Many of the designs still owed allegiance to earlier English manufacturers, but adaptions to local requirements gave the machines totally new aspects.

Most notable was the Crampton type, which earned widespread application in W. Europe from 1850 onwards for light high-speed express work. It corresponded to the English 'single-driver' period; Thomas Crampton was in fact English, but found only limited support in his homeland.

For heavy haulage 0-6-0 and 0-8-0 types were increasingly common. On steep grades even more coupled wheels were

desirable, but the limitations of curvature and rail strength precluded this. The developments of this requirement were the articulated locomotives pioneered by Mallet, Meyer and Haswell. Consequently all wheels could be used for adhesion, without damage to rails and within existing curve limitations.

Parallel to this was the development of Compounding, in which otherwise exhausted steam was reused in lower pressure cylinders. Pioneers were de Glehn and du Bousquet in France and Golsdorf in Austria. The process created powerful but essentially economic locos, but was eclipsed elsewhere by the introduction of super-heating and piston valves. However, compounding was developed in France right to the end of steam railways.

Centre: A PLM class C ('Windcutter') 4-4-0 four-cylinder de Glehn compound express locomotive circa 1894. The high pressure cylinders were mounted outside, whilst the larger low pressure cylinders were inside between the frames. Streamlining was added to the smokebox, chimney and cab-front, but how much this attributed to their maximum speed of 75 m.p.h. is debatable.

Lower right: Anatole Mallet patented a two-cylinder cross-compound in 1874, and built a series of diminu-tive 0-4-2T's for the Bayonne and Biarritz Railway to this patent in 1876. The first Mallet articulated, a small 0-4-4-0T, appeared in 1887. The true Mallet was a compound, with the low pressure cylinders on the for-ward truck. Illustrated is one of eight 0-6-6-0T's on the French Vivrais Railway from 1903. The last was withdrawn in 1967.

21

As in Britain, European rail systems were designed essentially to connect areas of mass population or industry. The grid pattern of rail links was nearing completion as the twentieth century dawned, and less accessible districts were being opened up. Isolated high-level Alpine townships, quarries, etc., were made more viable by various rack, adhesion and cable hauled systems, which in effect allowed locos to travel straight up mountainsides. Extremes of climate were overcome by effective steam-jacketting and condensing engines, to conserve heat and water respectively.

On the main lines locomotives were achieving power and size more in keeping with ever increasing traffic demands. Mallets were put to good effect on heavy freight services where speed was of lesser importance, but high sustained speeds on passenger services were being achieved by the earliest Pacific locos—the first in Europe being a de Glehn compound for the Paris-Orleans Railway in 1907. Less restrictive loading gauges allowed a greater and earlier adoption of large locos than in Britain, although shunting and branchline work were to continue to be handled by diminutive tank engines.

It would be incorrect to give an impression of constant smooth evolution of locomotive technology, but it would be true to indicate movements toward standardisation of locos and systems within and between the various nations. The best of what were previously piecemeal design improvements were brought together and re-analysed under controlled research conditions, but were still possibly subject to the personal preference of individual Chief Mechanical Engineers. Belpaire's flat-topped, narrow-based fire-box, Walschaert's radial valve gear, Golsdorf's steam distribution systems, Chapelon's 'inner streamlining', superheating, pre-heating, piston valves, poppet valves—all variously shaped links in a chain leading to a peak of development between 1920 and 1940.

Top left: On the Brienz-Rothorn Railway, an Abt system rack-and-pion locomotive, built 1891. Cogged driving wheels between the frames engaged two toothed rack rails for ascent and braking. The 'kneeling Cow' stance kept the firebox crown covered with water on steep slopes.

Centre left: Norwegian clas 27 4-6-0 built 1910-21, as two cylinder simple and four cylinder compounds. Light rail loadings were a major restriction in all Scandinavian countries. Note curious deflectors and combined sandbox/steamdome.

Lower left: Standard Prussian class T-9/3 2-6-0T in Belgian service. Large numbers of Prussian locos were acquired by Belgium as reparation after the Great War.

Centre below: Finest of the early Pacifics were those built for Bavarian State Railways by Maffei from 1908. They were four cylinder compounds, utilising the American-type wide firebox. The last of 159 were built by Henschel for the Reichsbahn in 1930.

Top right: RENFE 0-6-6-0 Mallet compound, formerly on the Central of Aragon line, built 1912 by Henschel.

Centre right: The Franco-Crosti boiler was a major economy measure that found limited support in most European countries. Exhaust was led back from the smokebox through 'economisers' finally passing out through chimneys just forward of the cab. Illustrated is a streamlined 2-6-2 example of Italian State Railways, fitted with Caprotti poppet valves, built 1927-40.

Lower right: Ultimate of the Abt system were Golsdorf's rack and adhesion locos built from 1912 for the Austrian Vordenberg line. Illustrated is one of two massive 2-12-2T's built under Deutsche Reichsbahn control in 1941 to Golsdorf's principles. In later years they were fitted with the superior Giesl exhaust ejector.

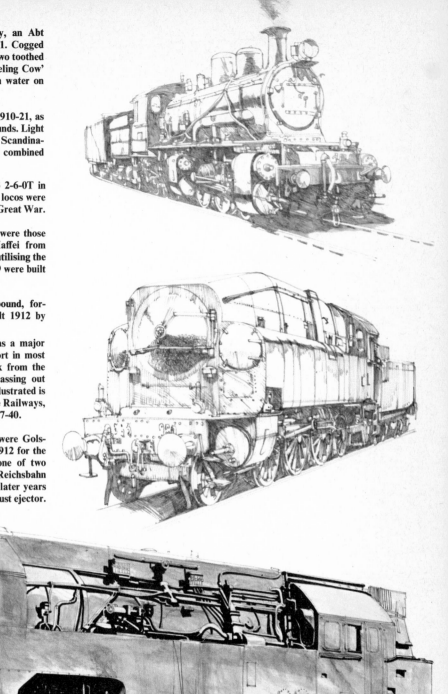

23

The aeroplane and motor car were impressing themselves more heavily into railway company profits by the 1920's, much as the railway companies themselves had done to canal and horse traffic almost a century earlier. Despite their lower capacities the aircraft and road vehicles were gaining prominence due to their speed and above all manoeuvreability. However, the position of most European railways was less critical than was the case with British companies, distances were greater and loads heavier—but had it not been for some timely and significant economic and prestigeous developments, especially for passenger traffic, then the final demise of steam might have come much earlier. Most important economic move was toward standardisation, cutting frills down to a minimum but allowing greater interchangeability of parts between classes and facilitating mass production. On the technical side Chapelon's internal refinements, especially of steam passages and front-ends, were to put every future locomotive designer in his debt. Guaranteed timetables, speed and running efficiency, not to mention improved passenger comfort, were to once again draw the public on to the railways.

Sadly the period was all too short-lived, for in the face of evidently superior diesel and electric traction, that elusive quality of economy, that the steam railway had constantly pursued or had been pursued by during its existence, was shortly to kill it.

Top left: Belgian class 12 streamlined Atlantic (4-4-2) for express passenger services between Brussels and Ostend from 1938. The air-smoothed casing was somewhat compromised to allow access to moving parts.

Top right: Streamlined de Caso designed Baltic (4-6-4) built for the Nord but incorporated into French National Railways (SNCF) from 1938. Of eight built three were three-cylinder simples, the rest four-cylinder compounds. The last was extensively modified by Chapelon and appeared in 1949.

Centre: For a time the world's fastest locomotive (124.6 m.p.h. in May 1936) 05.002 was one of three streamlined Baltics built by Borsig for the Reichsbahn in 1935. The 05.003 was designed to run cab-forward, using pipe-fed pulverised coal as fuel.

Below left: An ex Nord 2-10-0 four cylinder compound class 150.P, designed by Georges Collin. External design was typically rakish for this, the finest era of French steam. With a tractive effort of 56,500 lbs. they were designed to haul 2,000 ton coal drags on graded track, but were equally useful for fast passenger traffic.

Below right: Of all the railways in Europe, none followed the 'bare bones' approach to loco design so much as those of Germany, typified here by an example of the Bundesbahn's excellent class 50 2-10-0's; one of over ten thousand built in three classes 1927-49. Many were passed on to formerly occupied countries as reparation after World War Two and are to be seen in service to this day, especially in Eastern Europe.

The last locomotives built in Western Europe were ten Babcock and Wilcox Garratts for the RENFE in 1961. The Bundesbahn retains a full-overhaul policy for steam locos, so both West Germany and Spain will sport steam traction well into the 1980s. In Eastern Europe steam will survive longer, although new construction ended in 1968, but in view of the potential longevity of the steam locomotive, service should exceed the end of the century.

Top: Czechoslovakian heavy freight hauled by two 2-10-0s, the leading locomotive of typical German design, latterly the predominant influence in central Europe.

Centre: East German Reichsbahn 01.5 Pacific. 1968 construction, with welded boiler and firebox, Giesl ejector, Boxpok wheels and skyline casement.

Below: RENFE oil-burning 2-8-2 + 2-8-2 Garratt of 1961. Spain was the only European user of Garratt locomotives. The last ten were identical to five coal-burners of 1931.

AMERICA

Introduction

Below: Most distinctive of locomotive styling, the American, or 4-4-0 type, circa 1860. The pilot (cow-catcher), lamp and bell remained as standard equipment for American locomotives until the end. The diamond stack remained only so long as wood was burnt. Despite the ornate appearance of these machines they were extremely practical for their day, and were in fact rather rough and ready in structure, a feature easily recognisable in U.S. exports of Austerity steam locomotives many years later.

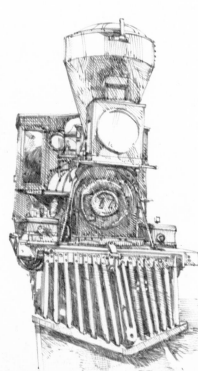

To a greater extent than in any other country, the American railroads were the arteries and veins along which the lifeblood of the nation flowed. In contrast to the old world, where the railway connected established areas of population, the towns and cities of the middle and western states were created by the railroad, and thus its historical importance is enhanced. The contrasts go deeper. In the U.S.A. ideas were, in general, more readily tried or rejected, in the accepted 'Pioneer' manner. Greater contrasts of distance, topography and traffic, of building practise, of organisational policy, all helped to create locomotives distinctly 'American' in character, and quite unlike the indigenous products of any other nation. Considering that within its boundaries the U.S.A. contained every extreme of railway environment, it is not surprising that it went on to become the premier influence on locomotive design elsewhere in the world.

Mechanical stokers, wide fireboxes, bar or cast frames, roller bearings, injectors, pre-heaters, all were typical late American practise. Front-end design was consistently poor, only in later years were such European measures as free-steam passages and double blast-pipes adopted—arising from an accent on power rather than on economy, arising in turn from a need to run heavy, infrequent, trains on single track or over steep gradients.

In the pioneer days design was by Norris Bros., Baldwin, Rogers, Winans and others of local or national importance. Few of the many railroad companies built their own stock. From the turn of the century construction was carried out by three major companies, Baldwin, Alco and Lima. Thus, as constructors came up with a new innovation, it would spread like a rash through the railroads, a periodic predominance of Pacifics, Hudsons, 4-8-4s etc, but in a slightly varied form for each company. Virtually alone, the Pennsylvania railroad remained a rebel, designing its own stock and rarely adopting the current fashion in locomotives.

Right: Col. Stevens 1824 locomotive, erected on a circular track in the grounds of his New Jersey home. A single cylinder drove a geared wheel onto a raised central rack rail. The vertical boiler was of the marine water-tube type, rated at an amazing 500 lbs. per sq. in. Stevens' son also figures prominently in the pioneer days of American railroads.

Above: American engineers were rarely satisfied with standard imported locomotives as supplied. This was a standard Stephenson 0-4-0 Samson type freight loco, first called Stevens, later John Bull, delivered to the Camden and Amboy in 1831. Poor riding on uneven track led to the fitting of a leading pilot, the first of its kind, to 'roll out the track'. The added cowled stack, lagged dome, bell and cab completed the transformation.

Characteristically, from the beginning the American locomotive was something unusual. Comparitively few locos were imported, and those that were, were soon adapted to local requirements. Roughly laid track took unkindly to large leading drivers more suited to carefully prepared roadbeds with no bumps or sharp curves, but with the addition of a leading pilot or full bogie such things became less important. Wood fuel called for a large chimney cowl to suppress glowing embers, bells were needed to warn both people and livestock on unfenced track—and a cow-catcher to remove those who failed to heed the warning in time.

Left: Stourbridge Lion, the first locomotive to run on an American public railroad, the Delaware and Hudson, in August 1829. It was imported from Britain by Horatio Allen, who was at the controls for the inaugural run. Unfortunately its weight far exceeded the safety limits of the track and a timber bridge en route, so one doubts if it's service was long.

The lobby for public railways started very early, chief advocate was Col. John Stevens, who built a locomotive to emphasise his point in 1824, but found little unified support. When railways did come the many small companies were even more of a confusion than their counterparts in Britain, and rolling rights were occasionally settled with loaded guns.

Above: John B. Jervis's 'Experiment' of 1832, with the pioneer sprung bogie. Note the continued use of European type outside sandwich frames, in production form bar frames were used, with Bury's haycock firebox and boiler. In 1836 Henry Campbell built a similar 4-4-0 for the Philadelphia and Norristown Railroad, the first of the American institution.

28

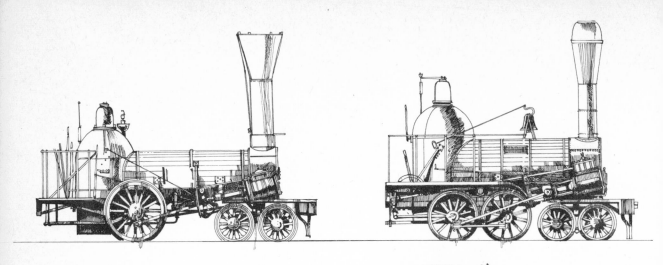

Above: Norris 4-2-0, circa 1835. The bar frame was initially adopted due to inadequate plate rolling facilities, whereas a frame built from bars could be put together by any competent blacksmith. Outside cylinders were universal. Norris 4-2-0 were generally freighters, Baldwin's, with drivers behind the firebox, improving stability at the cost of tractive effort, were generally passenger types.

Above right: 'Gowan and Marx', an early 4-4-0 (1839) of the Philadelphia and Reading Road. An anthracite-burner, it was intended for coal haulage on heavily graded lines. The extremely short wheelbase, therefore concentrated engine weight, allowed for exceptional tractive force. Weighing but 11 tons, it was capable of hauling 600 tons. Eastwick and Harrison, the constructors, later moved their business to Russia, but the Marx of the title had nothing to do with the later political theorist.

The 4-2-0 locomotives mark the point where America took a distinct and separate path of development. Anthracite burning, vertically boilered locomotives proved to be something of a long-lived dead-end. The leading bogie took care of uneven track, adequate tractive force came from single drivers near the centre of gravity and bar frames for strength without the weight penalty of plate frames, so the pattern was set for sixty years of development. The need for more tractive effort led naturally to the American Standard, or 4-4-0 type. From 1840 to 1870 the type was pre-eminent, its exploits in the civil war and far west now legend.

Above: A coal-burning (straight stack) 4-4-0 circa 1880, that served into the 1950s. After a short British period Canadian practice followed American ideals completely. Although the type was generally redundant by the 1890s, a big-boilered, big-wheeled New York Central 4-4-0, no. 999, was credited with 112 m.p.h. in 1893

Left: A typical 4-4-0, circa 1860. A principal for the type's longevity was the equaliser beam, which allowed the weight on each axle, including the bogie, to be varied according to differing track conditions and loads. Counterbalanced wheels minimised 'hammer-blow' on light track. Large sandboxes provided assistance to track friction. During this period standard gauge track superceded all others. Previously different gauges were adopted to suit the requirements of individual townships.

Above: First railway built purely for leisure effect, and the earliest of mountain lines—the Mt. Washington Cog—begun in 1869 and continuing to this day. Current services are operated by 'kneeling cows' of 1880 vintage.

Below: Baldwin 2-6-2 Saddle Tank for World War I service. This was for standard gauge, but many similar Pannier and Saddle tankers were built by Baldwin and Alco for 60 cm. frontline service. Mainline 2-8-0s were supplied for heavy freight, whilst at home the need for war materials led to the use of massive compound Mallets, attaining a 2-10-10-2 format on the Virginian.

Every country produced certain locomotives designed specifically for conditions peculiar to their shores, and rarely seen elsewhere. So it was in America. Lumbering, suburban services, industrial concerns etc., all required specialist locos, and peculiarities of fuel or water availability led to further unusual designs.

With the Great War, American locos appeared in Europe in large numbers. Apart from the later effect they had on local design, many so delivered remained in service long after hostilities ceased.

Railways were also exploited in the leisure field, special trains for World Fairs, scenic effects etc. Today this is the only capacity within America where steam holds strong and sadly is often debased in the pursuit of profits.

Right: Forney 0-4-4 for push-pull working on the New York Elevated railway. Such suburban services, although destructive of social amenities, were cheaper than underground, but still left ground level clear for road transport. Steam traction lasted from 1870 to 1900, when electric traction took over, steam being banned from the city.

Below: Three truck Shay geared loco, showing off-centre boiler to accommodate vertical cylinders alongside. This and the similar Heisler and Climax geared locos were the mainstay of logging roads from 1895 to recent times.

Below: The difficulty of fitting a normal cab to the wide Wootten anthracite firebox, led to the Camelback or Mother Hubbard, where the engineer's cab straddled the boiler, the fireman occupying the normal position. With early small boilers the engineer's position was a positive pavilion, but the growth of boilers reduced his accommodation, eventually resulting in the disappearance of this type. Illustrated is one of the three largest, -and only Mallet-Hubbards, 0-8-8-0 for Erie in 1906.

33

The 4-4-0 was a true mixed-traffic loco. Eventually freight loads exceeded the economic use of even double-heading, and were gradually taken over by 2-6-0, 2-8-0 and 2-8-2 types, from 1870, coinciding with overall increases in boiler and firebox dimensions.

The Mallet formulae from 1900 was rapidly stretched, so that each progressive articulated product was dubbed 'largest in the world'. A number of freaks were conceived en route, like the Santa fé, with flexible boilers as well as trucks—who were consequently put off articulation for all time. After reaching maximum size and power in the Great War period the compound Mallet went through a decline until the introduction of simple articulation in the 1930s.

Above: The most exceptional of the early giant Mallets, Southern Pacific's Cab Forwards, built in eleven classes 1909–44. Shown is a class AC-2 (formerly MC-2) 2-8-8-2, after conversion to simple expansion in 1930. As they burned oil the reverse format, with enclosed cab, was no problem to firing, and settled smoke clearance difficulties.

Below left: Although generally superceded by the popular 2-8-0, some Moguls laboured on short lines until the end, as witnessed by this East Jordan & Southern sample. Its form was typical of the turn of the century period.

Below right: Chesapeake & Ohio 2-6-6-2 compound Mallet, circa 1918. Note the large compound cylinders, and array of smokebox mounted air-brake pumps.

Above: Premier CP steam power, left to right: 2-10-4 Selkirk for Rockie mountain lines, 4-6-4 Hudson— semi-streamlined, and 4-6-2 Pacific. Various members of each type were streamlined, and all were used as mixed-traffic locos as a standardising measure.

Above right: Atchison, Topeka and Santa Fé 2-10-2 heavy freight. The classification was subsequently titled Santa fé. With retrospective superheating and mechanical stoking they represented a significant advance in loco engineering. Their form was typical of the bold and brash Baldwin lineage. After their removal from service in the early fifties their loads were taken on by diesel sets of up to five units in tandem.

Although capable of prodigeous haulage feats, compound Mallets were slow, and therefore, with high average speeds required, went through a decline in the 1920s. In their place rigid frame locos of up to ten coupled wheels were adopted. The Santa fé, never fond of articulation, had introduced the 2-10-2 in 1903. Their boilers were immense to provide constant supplies of steam, later improved by superheating. Larger fireboxes led to the 2-10-4 in the 'twenties, which also saw a revision to mixed traffic, with Lima's exceptional 2-8-4 (Berkshire). Curvature generally precluded any advance on five coupled axles, but Union Pacific adopted a 4-12-2 format in central Oregon, the 88 units built being adequate comment to its effectiveness. U.P. also provided the solution to the compound Mallet problem with its simple-expansion 4-6-6-4 Challenger class in 1936, which, with its 60 m.p.h. under heavy loads, largely eclipsed the long-frame freighters.

With its two major railroads, Canadian Pacific and Canadian National (Grand Trunk), loco practice north of the border was in all ways American. In the east British types were formerly common (a Hackworth 0-6-0 that ran until the 1890s is preserved in New-foundland), but in the west, and later throughout the Dominion, American derivatives reigned supreme. Latterly Pacifics, Hudsons and Selkirks were prime movers on the CP, with high-speed 4-4-4s on crack expresses, their equivalent of the Milwaukee Road Hiawatha Atlantics.

Below: Union Pacific class 9000 4-12-2. This large class provided a useful stopgap between the 2-8-8-0 compound and 4-6-6-4 Challenger simple artics. Fears of track damage due to such a long wheelbase proved baseless, although its service was mainly on the less curving Oregon section. Unusual in American practice the 9000s had three cylinders, with Gresley 2 to 1 gear for the centre valves. The tender was of the Vanderbilt type, with cast frame and cylindrical water tank. The UP was an Alco road, witnessed in the 9000's clean and uncluttered lines.

Below: The two extremes of twentieth century passenger haulage on the Pennsylvania road. The Pennsy Pacific, class K-4s, was an exceptional design for 1913, rather dated when production ended in 1931 after 425 units, and positively obsolete as it double headed its way into the 1950s. The M-1a was an excellent 4-8-2 mixed traffic derivation.

The T-1 Duplex was conceived as a solution to the dynamic augment (hammerblow) problem of big wheeled 4-8-4s. Drive was divided into two units in a rigid frame with smaller cylinders and lighter moving parts. In dividing the drive, however, tractive effort was considerably reduced, and wheelbase became inconveniently long. Fifty units were built from 1945, but all had disappeared by 1953. The 4-4-6-4 Q-2 freighter was also built in small numbers.

Left: Two of the 4-8-4 classics; top—Southern Pacific Class GS-4 Daylight of 1941, Lima built and oil-burning, boostered tractive effort 75,900 lbs. Centre— Canadian National U-2g, 203 units built from 1927. Tractive force 57,000 lbs.

Above: NYC Hudson class J-3a, as used on the crack Twentieth Century Limited, New York (Harmon) to Chicago. 961 miles in 18 hours, including thirteen stops, and curiously—a section through the main street of Syracuse at 10–15 m.p.h. Trailing bogie boosters assisted starting. The last ten appeared in Dreyfus-designed streamlining—good for publicity.

The limit of high-speed, big-wheeled, two-cylinder traction was reached with the 4-8-4, of which about thirty different types were incorporated into American roads. Axle loadings and hammer-blow forces were becoming intolerably high, and fuel consumption fantastic. The Pennsylvania's attempt to ammend the situation with the Duplex provided only half an answer, as indeed did similar experiments with steam turbines. Steam traction had reached its limit.

The final phase of American steam locomotives from the war to 1950 contained the most exceptional machines in the world. The Challenger types revolutionised both fast freight and heavy passenger traffic, and the logical development—the 4-8-8-4 'Big Boy' proved to be the largest and heaviest locos ever built. The Norfolk & Western, however, continued with compound Mallets to the end, including what was probably the world's most powerful loco. The N & W also made the last stand for steam against diesel/electric traction, succumbing in April 1960, thereby marking the final demise of steam traction in America.

Above: The NYC Niagaras were built as a direct challenge to diesel/electric capabilities in 1945. New York to Chicago they were able to accelerate 1,500-ton passenger stock to 85 m.p.h., consuming 100 tons of coal in the process.

Right: Built in 1952, the last N & W Y6b was scrapped in 1968, after only eight years' service on 15,000 ton coal drags, and eight years rotting in Roanoke, Virginia, waiting for the scrapper's torch.

Far right: Up class 4-8-8-4 Big Boy of the 1944 series, emphasising the displacement of the boiler on curves. Developing 8,000 h.p., their usual service was handling 5,000 ton freights over Sherman hill, Wyoming. Total weight exceeded 500 tons, for a length of 133 ft. 68 in. drivers gave a top speed of 70 m.p.h.

The South American states, like most of the countries covered in the concluding chapter, constructed very little of their total locomotive stock. Locos were acquired from the principal industrial countries, depending upon their suitability for local conditions—and occasionally upon the political aspirations of individual governments. Generally, however, the Ithsmus and N.W. South America came under the wing of the U.S.A., the remainder principally under British and German influences.

Top left: 4-6-2 + 2-6-4 Beyer Garratt for broad gauge Saõ Paulo Railway. Built as 2-6-2 + 2-6-2 in 1927, the five locos were the first true express Garratts. Conversion to double Pacifics in 1931 improved riding characteristics and increased water capacity.

Lower left: 1937 Henschel built simple expansion 2-8-8-4 Mallet for Central of Brazil, on metre gauge iron ore traffic. Fuel was lignite, mechanically stokered.

Gauges were many and various, ranging from 5 ft. 6 in. in Argentina to 3 ft. (as well as standard gauge) in Mexico. Garratts, entirely absent in N. America, were used in some profusion, as were Mallets, Meyers and Fairlies, and virtually every description of rigid frame loco. Railway's highest elevation was achieved, with normal traction, in Peru's La Cima pass at 15,848 ft. Oxygen was carried for the comfort of passengers.

Top right: Armstrong-Whitworth built 4-8-0 oil-burning freight loco for Buenos Aires Great Southern, 1924. Such orders made A-W, North British, Beyer-Peacock and other British constructors international names. 75 of these locos were built, principally for 2,000 ton fruit trains, and are still in service.

Lower right: A switching yard near Mexico City. Old wooden stock and primitive dual gauge track harkened back to pioneer American days. The locos shown were Baldwin outside frame 3 ft. gauge Mikados, similar to those used on the famous Rio Grande line. Working alongside these were powerful 4-8-4s, the equal of anything the great U.S. railroads could offer.

Introduction

With few exceptions the countries covered by the generality of this section were those formerly described as 'colonial'. In this sense they rarely designed or built indigenous locomotives, but had—by the dictates of their individual requirements—measurable influence on the products of the constructing countries. Initially such machines used were of identical design to those of the supplying country, but by the inevitable melting pot of other influences they took on an individual identity. As such they might be seen as better typifying the average of steam history, rather than the individual supplying nations.

Of special interest in this section, as the last major innovation of steam traction, and as a strictly 'colonial' machine, was the Garratt. Never used in N. America and only to a limited extent in Britain and Europe, it appeared in every country south of the Equator—and will probably be the last steam type to operate in revenue service anywhere in the world.

Below: Loading gauges had a greater effect on optimum locomotive development than rail gauges. From the left are shown the growth limits in America, Great Britain and South Africa. Note the similarity in size between the U.K. and S. African samples, despite the latter's narrow gauge track, and the great difference in size between locos from the U.K. and U.S.A., despite their common rail gauge. The apparently greater legroom beneath the British loco was due to standard platform heights, curiously a very early standard, and virtually unknown elsewhere.

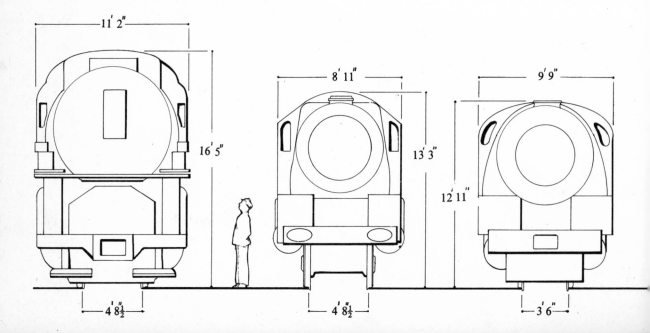

Right: A Norris 4-4-0 supplied to the Copiapo Railway, Chile, in 1850. This and the earlier 4-2-0 were America's first major export types. Evidently Chilean track conditions were comparable, if not worse, than contemporary American practice.

Below: The first Garratt, 0-4-0 + 0-4-0 for the Dundas Tramway, Tasmania, built by Beyer-Peacock, who held sole production rights, in 1909. Like the pioneer Mallets it was to say the least—small, running on 2 ft. gauge. Unlike subsequent Garratts this was a compound, with cylinders on the inner ends of the bogies connected by a steam pipe. The designer, H. W. Garratt was formerly a railway inspector in Australia. He died in 1913, with only a few of his locomotives in service.

Opposite top: Pre-revolution Russian types included large numbers of Fairlies and Mallets. Most burned oil or wood. The first conversion of a Mallet to simple expansion took place in Russia in 1903, apparently much to the originator's displeasure.

Centre: The most numerous locomotive, the E type 0-10-0, of which over 13,000 units were built 1912–52.

Bottom: The last mainline design built in quantity, the P.36 4-8-4 of 1950, 250 of which were drawn into stock before production ceased in 1956.

Below: Soviet class FD 2-10-2 as supplied to China from 1958. 2000 of this class were earmarked for conversion, but less than half were actually delivered. However, complete drawings of the similar but superior class L 2-10-2 were passed on, and these locomotives may have been constructed locally.

Bottom: Last British deliveries to China were of these simple but effective 0-8-0 banking engines, 1950. The massive firebox was designed to burn low quality fuel. 13 ton axle load gave them wide route availability.

Contradicting the opening statements of this chapter, Russia was in no way a colony of any other nation, and therefore, retained an identity of its own, largely insulated from outside influences. Consequently there was nothing quite like a Russian locomotive. Rail gauge was 5 ft., with a loading gauge that exceeded 17 ft. height, and allowed the carriage of cars two abreast in special wagons. Characteristically with a railway entirely state owned, there were few different locomotive classes at any one time, but each was built in large numbers. From 1930 new designs were distinctly American-inspired, and continued in that mould to the end.

At the opposite end of the scale, China's railways were completely colonial in character, but this did not prevent them operating exceptionally advanced locos. The 1934 Vulcan 4-8-4 for the Canton-Hankow line was in every sense a masterpiece. Latterly, with the introduction of a communist government, western supplies dried up, to be replaced by Russian locos, suitably converted to standard gauge—virtually Russia's only locomotive exports. Since the idealogical split of the mid-60s these supplies have also dried up, and little is known of current railway practice.

Above: Two Japanese National Railways locos; class C62 4-6-4, the last JNR type, fifty of which were built 1948–49, the last retired in 1972. 2-8-0 freighters were built in large numbers 1913–26, before American design influence took hold. Several survive as yard switchers.

Above right: Two stages in New Zealand's loco development, on the left a Nielson 2-6-0 class J, circa 1880. On the right, a Kb 4-8-4, the optimum development of N.Z. steam power, home designed and built at Hutt Valley works 1931–50.

With Japan's railways laid to 3 ft. 6 in. gauge, JNR steam locos gave the impression of giants on tightropes. A late starter, Japan has only recently passed a century of rail travel. However, later Hudsons and Mikadoes were equal to their task, and still serve in large numbers, especially on the N. Island, Hokkaido.

Australian railways contained many contrasts due to a chaotic three-gauge system, and individual rolling policy in each of the six states. Only since 1970 has through working east-west been possible, whilst the north-south 3 ft 6 in. link was dropped with 600 miles between the track ends. Garratts still operate in Queensland and New South Wales, but current motive-power comes from U.S.-built or inspired diesel sets.

New Zealand's mountainous landscape, although picturesque, made communal links of any kind difficult. The pioneers, recognising the need for railways, made a concession to nature by limiting the loading gauge to a height of 11 ft. 6 in., a width of 8 ft. 6 in., with 3 ft. 6 in. track and max. axle loadings of 14 tons. As a result the Kb 4-8-4, the last major design, was a masterpiece of compact engineering, boosting tractive force to 36,000 lbs. and a top speed of 65 m.p.h.

Below: Left to right; NSW C38 Pacific, thirty of which were built locally 1941–43, the first five as streamliners, one of which is preserved in running order; NSW AD60 4-8-4 + 4-8-4 Beyer-Garratt, largest and most powerful Australian loco, 125 ft. long, 63,000 lb. tractive effort. 42 were built by Beyer-Peacock 1952–57; South Australian Railways class 520 4-8-4, twelve built 1943–44 for 5 ft. 3 in. gauge. The streamlined shape was derived directly from the Loewy-designed Pennsylvania T.1 Duplex.

'Colonial' could best be applied to the African states, most W. European countries formerly possessing territories in the continent. Gauges were many and varied, but mostly in the metre and 3 ft. 6 in. range. The most extensive and consistent steam development took place in S. Africa. Generally of British and German manufacture, with strong U.S. influence every major steam advance being covered. Garratts were (and still are) prominent, especially south of the equator. Since the demise of U.S. giants, the East African Railway's 59th class 4-8-2 + 2-8-4s are currently the world's largest locomotives. Recent political upheavals in E. Africa have had a lot to do with railway developments, and although electrification proceeds apace, it is probable that these steam giants will be serving well into the 21st century.

Above: Representative of articulated types: Left; SAR class G CA 4-8-2 + 2-8-4 Garratt, Krupp built in 1927. The GL class of 1929 remains the most powerful narrow gauge type in the world, almost 80,000 lbs. tractive effort. Centre; Rhodesia Railways 20th class of 1954. Until the troubles of 1973, such locos headed coal and iron-ore traffic across the Zambesi to and from Zambia. Right; Ugandan 0-6-6-0 compound Mallet, North British built for metre gauge in 1913.

Far left: German-built 2-10-2 of Mozambique Railways, connecting with the Rhodesian system for freight traffic.

Below: Ultimate development in S. Africa, class 25 4-8-4, with Henschel condensing tender for bad water districts.

Above, from the right: Standard 2-8-0 of Bengal
Nagpur circa 1912. The type appeared on every Indian
broad gauge line; Class YD 2-8-2 for metre gauge
Burma State Railways 1927–48, broad gauge Indians
received the X classification; Broad gauge WP
Pacific of the unified Indian State Railway, delivered
1957 from Canada. Note distinctive bullet nose.

India became the British Empire's exercising ground for numerous
'standard' systems of varying success, largely moulded in the
typical British vein. The last standard, classes WP (4-6-2) and
WG (2-8-2) for passenger and freight traffic respectively, were
American influenced and initially Canadian built. Orders were
placed in 1970 for further WGs from Chitteranjan workshops—
India, with its population and work-shortage problems, having no
need of the manpower saving with diesels. However, outside of the
possibilities yet to be uncovered in Communist China, these must
surely be the last new steam locos.

**Above: A Merryweather 0-4-0 steam tram of the
North London Tramway Co. 1885–89.**

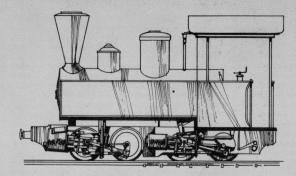

The pioneer Mallet of 1887, a diminutive 0-4-4-0 with inside and outside frames and compound cylinders. Its gauge was 2 ft., and wheelbase only 9 ft.

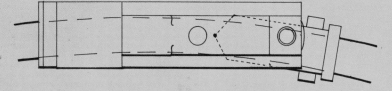

The last Fairlies were those of Pechot-Bourdon for the French Military Railways in the Great War. The limited firebox between the two boilers was a principle factor that precluded any extensive development.

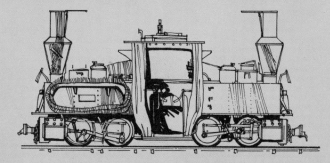

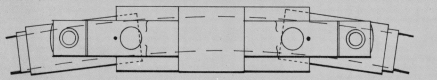

The sole outside frame 2-4-0 + 0-4-2 2 ft. 6 in. gauge Beyer Garratt of Ceylon Government Railways, built in 1929. Despite the gauge limitation, the total unit was over forty feet long.

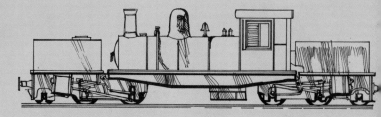

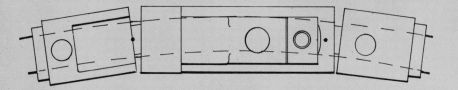